The Gift of Personal Writing

Reflective Writing for
Pleasure, Peace of Mind, and Personal Growth

Melinda L. Ferguson

ISBN: 978-1-7373746-1-9

Cover and interior designed by Diana Wade
Author photo by Jeanine Boubli

Printed in the United States of America

Published by Wirt Publishing

Better to write for yourself and have no public,
than to write for the public and have no self.

Cyril Connolly

♥ *To My Daughters & My Muses*
Katharine
Lindsey
Allison

Contents

Introduction   1

1. A Quick-start Guide to Keeping a Journal   5

2. Some Notions on What to Write About   17

3. How to Protect Your Privacy   39

4. Finding Times & Places to Write   45

5. Writing for Healing, Health, & Wholeness   51

6. Reading and Re-Viewing Old Journals   61

7. Journal Writing in the Classroom   65

8. Where Do Your Journals Go When You Die?   67

9. Epilogue   71

10. A Book of My Own   73

Acknowledgments   83

About The Author   87

Introduction

*J*ournal writing rewards individuals of every age and background. You don't have to be a poet, writer, or an artist to keep a journal, which was a misapprehension I held for decades. I believed keeping a journal was a pastime for geniuses or the idle rich, a far too grand and time-consuming pastime for a practical person like me. Instead, I have learned over the past 30-some years that journal writing is a means of integrating your unique physical, mental, and spiritual perceptions while, at the same time, tapping into your creativity. Journaling also helps you organize daily life.

I started to keep a journal, a "Mother's Journal," after my third child was born. The family had moved from Manhattan to a small town on Long Island, and I was to become a full-time mother and homemaker. My purpose was to prize motherhood and to record my daughters' childhoods. I wanted to preserve family memories. Our lives were so busy, I could barely recollect what happened from one day to the next. Today my daughters are grown and have children of their own, and my journals are more precious to me than ever. In addition to the sheer pleasure of reliving those days, I'm convinced revisiting the past is good for my health because my words keep the memories alive.

Not long after starting my first journal, I realized that writing down my thoughts and feelings and recording family stories was having an amazing positive effect on me. Writing was clearly something that rewarded me with a better sense of myself, with a keener eye for observing nature, and with an ever-expanding awareness and gratitude for the gift of life itself. I became more self-aware and more understanding of others' points of view.

I've written this book because I know that journal writing changes lives. Over the years, I have assigned journaling to hundreds of students, from aged eighteen to eighty-five: young people taking developmental writing classes; young, middle-aged and older adults enrolled in introductory freshman English classes; all levels of English as a Second Languages classes. I've also taught journal and memoir writing workshops to adults seeking to discover the patterns in their lives, to trace where they came from, how they got to where they are today, and where they wish to go from here. Given the freedom to write thoughts and feelings without fear of making mistakes, of being judged or corrected, writers of all ages gain confidence in their abilities to think critically, to express themselves honestly, and to appreciate the complexities of the English language. Perhaps best of all, you, the journal-keeper, get to write when, where, and what you wish, at your own pace.

While writing school essays is difficult, keeping a journal is easy. You don't exert yourself; instead, you relax while you scribble your thoughts, feelings, memories, and dreams. You are "doing" and "being" simultaneously. You settle into a comfortable chair or couch to write about the things you know and the things you wonder about. Minutes later, when you finish your entry and return to the world, you still have a mile-long to-do list, but you feel stronger and more in control of your life. You've sorted things out a bit, you've taken account of your inner life, that part of you that no one ever sees. You are refreshed. It's as if time somehow expanded; you know what to do next. You have not wasted your time.

No one judges what you write in your personal journal — not even, and *especially* not, you! You don't have to have what are considered "good writing skills." In fact, caring about handwriting, spelling, conventional rules of grammar and so on may actually get in the way of being spontaneous and straightforward.

You are free to style your journal in your own inimitable way. Make your book an original: you might decide to write right to left, upside down and backward, in code, in another language or in a made-up language of your own; you might draw pictograms and sketches to illustrate your words.

In the back of this book, you'll find blank pages entitled "A Book of My Own." Experiment with these pages after you've read my suggestions. Practice expressing yourself and exploring your own mind. The challenge is this: Use up the blank pages, then draw your own conclusions. You have nothing to lose and much to gain. If you feel rewarded by the practice of reflective writing, you will have fun searching for the right kind of journal for you (see Chapter 1). If journal writing isn't your "thing," you will take away an important experience that may motivate you to search until you find the right activity for you that will gift you with pleasure, peace of mind, and personal growth.

If you can't be a friend to yourself,
how can you be a friend to anyone else?
Eleanor Roosevelt

1

A Quick-start Guide to Keeping a Journal

There are many reasons you will enjoy, and be rewarded by, keeping a journal. Begin here:

- Give yourself permission to write spontaneously.
- Set aside time to write daily, or as often as possible.
- Defeat your fear of writing.

These are challenging undertakings not to be underestimated. But with time, practice, and patience, you will learn that personal writing is a tool for better living. You will discover that even a one-minute check-in with your journal is worth the effort. And best of all, when you overcome your fear of writing and learn to express yourself more confidently in your journal, you will also be able to express yourself better in relationships with others.

All you need really is a journal, a couple of pens, and a timer. But also, think about your journaling practice with a hospitable mind. Treat your writing self with the attention and consideration that you would give a much-loved friend who comes to visit. Choose the best place to sit, one with the most beautiful view in the house – perhaps near a window, where you can look out upon trees or a patch of sky, a lawn, lake, garden, or flowerpot. Before you sit down, open the window for a breath of fresh air if the weather permits, and offer yourself a cup of tea or coffee. You may want to light a candle or burn incense to set these moments apart from the rest of your busy day.

Relax. Curl up into your favorite chair, or prop your feet up on an ottoman. If it's chilly, wrap up in a soft sweater and toss a throw over your legs and feet. Adjust a cushion to support your back. Attending to the details of your physical comfort is not a waste of time. How we feel affects how and what we think.

Set a timer for five minutes or more—whatever you can spare. Open your journal and pick up a pen. Have a second pen within easy reach so your writing time will not be interrupted by the need to search for a replacement. Write the date at the top of the page. Note the time. In a couple of words, describe the weather ("cool and overcast") and your immediate environment ("on the deck, enjoying flashes of sunshine"). Take a deep breath. Can you identify a pleasant scent, or an awful odor? What do you see, what do you hear in and around your home? Are you enjoying the taste of your beverage? Are your hands cold? Is your knee bothering you again? Are you feeling snug and safe?

By taking your time and paying close attention to your world, including physical sensations, you develop your powers of observation and consciousness. Having oriented yourself, you're prepared to cross the bridge from your shared and observable world to your inner life. In the pages of your journal, you will capture your unique thoughts, feelings, memories, and creativity.

Don't think! Write!
Madeleine L'Engle

What you have to say and the way you say it is perfect. Let the words flow without interruption through your hand to the pen to the page. Imagine your thoughts moving along as a fast-flowing stream—a creek coursing over rocks and around boulders. Let the rushing waters carry away self-doubts. Your voice is neither more nor less important than anyone else on this planet, and, as a unique individual, you have valuable things to say. Our world will be a better place for your having made your voice heard, even if only on the page.

These suggestions for how to begin keeping a journal are my methods that have worked for years for me and my students. You should feel free to develop your own journal writing practices over time, practices modified according to your individual preferences and life circumstances. For example, if you are a working mom or dad, your time for yourself is scant, but if you are a retiree, you may have greater freedom to choose when and for how long to write.

The important thing is to own your journal; "own" it by taking charge of your practice and building on it over time. It is never too late to start, and your future self will thank you.

Tools for Writing

Organizing is what you do before you do something,
so that when you do it, it is not all mixed up.
A.A. Milne

◇◇◇◇◇◇◇

To both energize and maintain your stream of thought as you write, bank on organization. A river moves swiftly, in part, because of its banks; a river without banks is called a swamp. If everything you need is together in a drawer, box, basket, on a shelf or tucked into tote bag, you will not waste a precious moment searching for something. Consider keeping tape, scissors, notepaper, and a small stapler in your toolbox, too, in case you want to cut out a picture or quotation from a magazine and fix it into your book.

Before launching into the actual writing, let's pause to consider the tools you need to assure a successful experience: Paper, Pen, and Timer. You may want to start with familiar products you have on hand, so make use of what you have; for example, an old notebook or a journal you've abandoned and the nearest available pencil or pen. When it's time to invest in something new, investigate the array of writing products available.

Years ago when I was a kid, my dad taught me how to enjoy shopping at a hardware store by carefully evaluating and comparing brands. "You can do a good job faster with the right tools," he said. "Good tools make a hard job easier." It's one of life's small delights to discover exactly the right tools for you.

Now, online shopping for almost anything is likely to introduce you to a literal world of products. But, in addition to cybershopping, you will have fun getting away from your computer and exploring inspiring selections of blank books and pens in business, office, art supplies, and gift stores, as well as independent and national bookstore chains. Over the years, I've often stocked up on beautiful blank books at discount department stores.

Well begun is half done.
Aristotle

How to Choose a Journal

*T*o maximize your enjoyment, select a journal that is attractive, suited to your needs, and affordable. You want to look forward to journal writing, so select a book that invites you, that beckons you, to settle down and pick it up. You do not want to be annoyed by a book that is too small, too large, or too heavy for your purposes, or a binding that will not open flat, or pages that bleed ink. You don't want to buy a journal that is so expensive you'll be afraid to write in it, or one so cheap that the pages fall out.

There is an ever-growing selection of journals to suit all budgets and tastes. What kind of book attracts you and feels good in your hands? A large artist's portfolio with pages for doodling, sketching, collage, or calligraphy? A take-it-any-where style that slips into a shirt pocket or small handbag? Something in between? A plain cover, a decorative fabric cover, or a hand-made, hand-sewn paper cover? A leather-covered journal with a rustic binding and hand-sewn pages has a whiff of adventure about it. Can you picture yourself writing in an elegant book with a kid-leather cover, golden-edged pages, and a satin ribbon bookmark?

Ask yourself: Will you write at a desk or table, or will you prop your journal on your lap? Compare the advantages of a spiral binding and a perfect binding (a book with a rigid spine). Spiral-bound books allow a writer to open the book to lie flat on a surface or to fold it in half on his or her lap.

If you travel frequently, you will want to consider portability. Will you want your journal stowed in carry-one luggage or in checked bags? If you are a frequent walker, you may want a journal you can stash in a shirt or pants pocket. Famous, compact Moleskin journals come in a variety of styles and sizes with handy features such as a small pocket in the back for storing cards, ticket stubs, or photos. Leather journals with refillable pages are also popular with travelers. Because of their uniform size, the inserts require minimum shelf space to store. Other options to consider are small, often beautifully illustrated paperback journals, frequently sold in three-packs. These are lightweight, versatile, and perfect for recording a particular event, such as a trip or vacation.

The most simple, easy to store, and least expensive kinds of journals are spiral-bound stenographers' notebooks, and marbled-covered school composition notebooks. For some writers, loose-leaf paper stored in a three-ring binder or a manila file folder is a practical choice.

Remember to examine the quality of paper in your journal. Most paper that is bound into blank book absorbs ink well, but some contain inexpensive pages that cannot hold ink. Consequently, the ink shows, or bleeds, through to the reverse side of the page and renders it useless.

How to Choose a Pen

The pen is the tongue of the mind.
Miguel de Cervantes Saavedra

Have you ever experimented with different kinds of pens? Fountain pens? Ballpoints? Felt-tipped? Gels? Fine point, medium point or broad tipped? Is your hand more comfortable when you hold a large-barreled pen, or do you prefer a slender one? You need a pen that does not cause your hand to cramp and that glides almost effortlessly across the page. You do *not* want a faulty pen that will interrupt your thoughts. Few things are more exasperating that losing your train of thought because a pen skips or skids to a stop, inkless.

Investigate a variety of pens at a nearby art supplies or business products store. Test your grip on a variety of styles and sizes, and write your name or a sentence or two before you make a purchase.

While you are at the store, try out different colors of ink. You might find it's fun to write purple prose. When I sit down to write, I enjoy having a selection of colored inks to choose from.

When I started my first journal, I wrote with a pencil. I intended to go back over what I'd written and erase mistakes. This notion was delusional. I barely had time to write, never mind to edit and revise what I wrote.

I came to realize that, for me, using a pencil was inhibiting. I was too self-conscious and wrote in fear of making a mistake. On top of that anxiety, I felt obligated to make corrections, as if I were writing a school essay. When you write in your journal, you are free of every rule you ever learned. Have fun! You are not writing a textbook.

An Indispensable Item for your Toolbox: a Timer.

I discovered the timer trick by happenstance, standing at the kitchen stove waiting for pasta to cook. It suddenly it hit me: This was <u>the</u> last opportunity of the day to start my journal. Right here and right now, before dinner and while the girls were watching their television show. After our meal and the evening routine and chores, I would be too tired to remember much of what had happened, and most certainly would not have the energy to write about it.

My oldest daughter had just had her first day of school! Earlier in the day, I'd <u>promised</u> myself for the umpteenth time I would keep a journal chronicling family life. I had to write <u>something</u> about this special day.

"Begin <u>now</u>!" I said to myself. I fetched a pencil and my *Mothers Journal* that I'd bought two years earlier, set the timer for 12 minutes, and got to work at the kitchen counter.

For the first time in my life, I wrote without thinking, without pausing to wonder what I should say or how I should say it. There was no time to suffer paralysis by analysis. I gave no thought to paragraphs or sentences and was possessed by a single urgent idea: "Write! Time's a-wasting!"

Had I not captured then, in a few words, the delight and details of that special day in the lives of my family, I wouldn't be able to look back and enjoy the memory years later.

◇◇◇◇◇◇◇

I'm late! I'm late for a very important date!
No time to say
"Hello" – goodbye! I'm late I'm late!
I'm late!
The White Rabbit, Alice in Wonderland

◇◇◇◇◇◇◇

Setting a timer will enhance your journal writing practice by helping clear your mind of other responsibilities so that you can concentrate on what you have to say. If you are preoccupied by a task, such as being worried about picking up your daughter at soccer practice, you cannot give your full attention to your journal.

When you sit down to write, ask yourself: "Can I spare five minutes? Twenty minutes?" Decide, and set your timer accordingly. You have given yourself permission to step back from your daily duties and check-in with yourself, fully aware of how much time you have and certain you'll be reminded when to stop. In short, you'll have peace of mind. When you close your journal and return to your everyday commitments, you'll be energized to take on the next task.

Don't watch the clock. A preoccupation with time – how many minutes do I have left? – is a distraction that will prevent you from writing freely.

Keep a slovenly, headlong, impulsive, honest diary .
. . .
I don't mean a "had lunch" diary. But do this:
write every day or as often as you possibly can,
as fast and carelessly as you possibly can, without
reading it again, anything you happened to have
thought, seen or felt the day before. In six months
look at it . . . . You will see that what you have
written with the most slovenly freedom – in those
parts there will be vitality, brilliance, beauty.

Brenda Ueland

2

Some Notions on What to Write About

Nothing is more important than this day.
Johann Wolfgang von Goethe

*I*n her diary, Anne Frank adopted the practice of addressing an imaginary friend, Kitty, to whom she confided her innermost secrets as well as the everyday details of her life. Your journal is your best friend, whether you give it a name or not. Nothing is too big or too small to record and reflect upon, so whatever comes to mind is worth mentioning. You're writing a book with an audience of one—yourself— and have the freedom to talk about whatever you please.

Below are eighteen suggestions to get you started. Try a variety of prompts to learn which work best for you. Once you've established your own ritual, you will instinctively select the subject you want or need to write about.

1. What day is it?

Does today mark a holiday, a big event, an anniversary or a milestone in your life? Is it someone's birthday? Take note of the occasion and what memories it evokes, or what you might do to make the day special. Most of us keep a calendar of private memories, too. Poet Henry Wadsworth Longfellow describes these days as "anniversaries of the heart".

> *The holiest of all holidays are those*
> *Kept by ourselves in silence and apart,*
> *The secret anniversaries of the heart…*

Your journal is a place to honor personal and private memories.

2. Paint a detailed word picture of the view outside your window.

In a written description, you will come to "see" your surroundings in a new way. Relate sensory details as specifically as you can; paint a word picture of the scene and how it makes you feel.

3. Identify an object or picture that is of value to you.

Look around the room where you're writing and identify an item that is special to you in some way. What is the story behind that object? How and under what circumstances did you come to possess it? Who gave it to you? In the future, you may choose to gift that memento to someone you believe would appreciate it as much as you do. Write a note to him or her describing what the object means to you, and why.

4. Take note of your health

Are you suffering with a nagging pain that won't go away? Perhaps worried about what might be the cause, yet afraid to know? You don't want to complain because your loved ones would worry. Tell your journal the whole story! List your worries. In the future, if you do see a doctor, the journal will be of help to her in diagnosing and treating you because you'll be able to say when you first noticed something "different," when you developed symptoms, and what changes and patterns you observe.

5. What are you doing today?

Do you feel overwhelmed with things to do, or are you bored and restless?

Write about all the appointments, chores, tasks you have to do, but not just a bullet list. The to-do list is useful, but to sort out your priorities, to identify the essential, possible, and aspirational ambitions of your day, it helps to add some details to remind yourself why something must be done. You'll find peace of mind taking a few minutes to bring order to the day, to describe your choices and determine what is essential.

On the other hand, if you find yourself believing "there's nothing to do," think back to your childhood memories. How did you have fun when you were a kid? Look for ways you can renew your interests today; for example, volunteer to coach or become a literacy tutor. Who were your best childhood friends? Consider reconnecting with an old friend with a phone call or writing a note, or plan a trip to revisit favorite people and places.

6. Are you feeling a particular sense of relief, joy, or gratitude today?

Are you or a loved one recovering from an illness? Do you feel blessed by a new opportunity, a promotion at work, or a supportive spouse and loving family? Express your gratitude in your journal. You may feel prompted to write a note of appreciation.

7. Catalog everything that you are thankful for.

It will make you happy. Since ancient times, eminent minds have recognized the value of a thankful spirit. "Gratitude is not only the greatest of virtues, but the parent of all others," wrote Cicero. No matter how many worries and woes in life, there is beauty, goodness, and love to help us find our way if we look for it. Taking a moment to be thankful refreshes our spirits and neutralizes negativity.

Gratitude unlocks the fullness of life. It turns what we have into enough, and more. It turns denial into acceptance, chaos to order, confusion to clarity. It can turn a meal into a feast, a house into a home, a stranger into a friend. Gratitude makes sense of our past, brings peace for today, and creates a vision for tomorrow.
Melody Beattie

Typically, I write early in the morning, but I learned to list things I was thankful for in the evening before turning out the bedside lamp. It helped me sleep to recall the gratifying moments of the day. I found it most useful to make every individual item a full sentence, a complete idea, beginning with "I am thankful for…" The rhythm of those words was soothing and seemed to help me remember.

> *Saturday, April 13 10:30 pm Bedroom*
>
> *I am grateful today for junk day, and the debris that is gone from my life*
>
> *I am thankful for having work to do*
>
> *I am thankful for the coldish gray rainy day to water the garden*
>
> *I am thankful for the fresh strawberries cut, sugared, and chilled, stored in a Tupperware container, ready for breakfast for the girls and their overnight guests.*
>
> *I am thankful for hearing from my longest-best friend, Jan.*
>
> *I am thankful for writing, which has helped me or perhaps enabled me to survive the crises of my life.*

8. The Twenty-Four-Hour Review

This is an infallible way to begin a journal entry and a fallback option if you don't know what else to write about.

When you are ready and know how much or how little time is available, take a deep breath, close your eyes, and picture where you were and what you were doing exactly twenty-four hours ago. Open your eyes and begin the story of the last twenty-four hours. Write fast. Trust the memories that come to mind and keep your hand moving across the page.

Do not worry about accurate sequencing. Don't think, "How can I cover 24 hours in so little time?" because, obviously, you cannot. What will emerge, whenever you are telling the story of your life that day, is what you recall most vividly. You're not trying to record the all the facts of the day. Self-discovery is what reflective writing is all about; you learn about yourself by paying attention to what you remember.

*How we remember, and what we remember, and
why we remember form the most personal map of
our individuality.*
Christina Baldwin

When your timer sounds, stop. Usually you'll feel a little tension for having stopped abruptly. Take a second to jot a word or two about what you still want to mention. Later, if you have time, pick up your journal and complete your thoughts.

Your reflections might give you a bit of a jolt. Imagine that the event of the day on your calendar was a dreaded dentist appointment, and you expected to write about that. Instead, what you write about is how, on your way to the dentist, you were sitting impatiently at a traffic light and randomly "your" song, shared with your high school sweetheart, who's now a dentist, blasts through the air from the car idling in the next lane. How weird is that? Perhaps you didn't even mention the root canal you endured?

9. Weep and Gnash your Teeth

Practice your right to whine, worry, complain, and vent. Your journal is a place to dump guilt and regrets including everything you've ever said or done that you wish you hadn't, and everything you wish you had said or done, but didn't. Here you have license to violate admonitions that many of us might have learned too well. For example, "Everybody has problems. Don't burden other people with yours." Your journal isn't other people. Unburden yourself in your book.

Another example of an aphorism to ignore in your journal: "If you can't say something nice, don't say anything at all." Say what you truly think, whether in hot-tempered haste or cool, measured analysis. Let it go and pour it all out on the page. You can revisit your thoughts at a later time and decide if you've changed your mind.

"No whining!" Violating this favorite parental command is entirely acceptable in your journal. Whine as much as you want about anything and everything that bothers you. You cannot stand your boss or a colleague? Your nosy neighbor? Get these things off your chest and onto pages that can absorb your frustration and anger. You are doing yourself a favor by releasing tension in a safe place on the page. Once you've expressed your emotions, and if you find yourself repeating the same complaints time and again, you might be able to see a person or situation more objectively and discover reasonable ways to change, or tolerate, the circumstances. At the same time, you are doing your family, friends, and colleagues a favor by not taking your frustration out on them.

Over the years, I became more respectful of what initially I regarded as my petty complaints and self-pity. I changed. If something bothered me, that "something" deserved my attention.

> *Wednesday, May 19 7:35 am*
>
> *I'm feeling cranky and in spite of all I say and believe about journal writing, it is hard for me to say that—and even to say why. I don't want to be misunderstood. My complaints and concerns are a spec on the canvas of my life as it unfolds each day—not worth noticing or noting, not worth the trouble, time, or ink. Yet insignificant as my troubles are, they are also part of my truth. I ought not push them aside to the wings without letting them take a bow on the stage. Even minor characters ought to be recognized. They're part of the picture, part of what's going on.*

10. Detect moments during a day that make you happy.

When life is at its most hectic, finding satisfaction in a few moments of pleasure or just a time-out widens your perspective. Know what the highlights of your day are so you can also enjoy anticipating them.

Years ago, I named my time-outs the "Pillars of the Day" and made up a game—a mash up of tic-tac-toe and bingo. Each morning, especially on those days I knew would be challenging, I drew a tic-tac-toe board in my journal and wrote one "pillar" in each square. The object was to "win" at least one game (crossing out three squares, as in tic-tac-toe), but my hope was to win the entire board, crossing out the nine squares. Early on, my pillars were (1) Quiet cup of coffee; (2) Read newspaper; (3) Stretching exercises; (4) Write a letter to a friend; (5) Journal (always in the middle of my game board); (6) Take a walk; (7) Afternoon quiet time; (8) Tea and snack with the kids; (9) Listen to/Play Music.

I regarded marking three squares as a victory, but my family were winners, too, because, after a little self-care, I was more fun to be with.

Your moments will be different, of course. The important thing is to be aware of when you are "having fun" in your own way.

11. Take Credit Where Credit is Due

When my children were in school full-time, I concocted in my journal a Family Game to remind me what my job was, meaning, what was most important for the well-being of my family. It was gratifying at the end of the day to check off items with a fat blue marker.

In part, I made up this checklist to teach myself to take a little credit for a day well spent. After all, as Mom and Homemaker, I spent a lot of energy and time performing jobs that I tended to shrug off because none of the tasks seemed important. In fact, most days it seemed that no one paid much attention to what I did day-to-day unless I didn't do it!

My list has changed over the years. These are examples from the years when my kids were all in elementary school:
1. Did they go off to school in clean clothes, combed hair, brushed teeth?
2. Did they eat a good breakfast?
3. Did they make their beds before they left?
4. Was their schoolwork done?
5. Did we pack nutritious lunches and snacks?
6. Did we have an enjoyable family supper?
7. Did I spend some one-to-one time with each child?
8. Did I read to each child?

Yes? Bingo! Take a bow! It was a very good day.

12. Dreams

Our dreams are rich sources of knowledge and inspiration. When you are awakened by a dream—or a nightmare—during the night, write it down as quickly as possible before you forget. Then borrow a line from

Scarlett O'Hara and say to yourself, "I can't think about that right now. If I do, I'll go crazy. I'll think about that tomorrow." Go back to sleep.

If, in the morning you awaken with a dream, scribble down the story, the characters, the images and every detail you recall as fast as possible, without trying to interpret anything. Don't fret about its meaning. Later—and perhaps it will be years later, when you re-read your journal—you will discover meanings you could never have imagined.

*I've dreamt in my life dreams that have stayed
with me ever after, and changed my ideas. They've
gone through and through me, like wine through
water, and altered the color of my mind.*
Emily Brontë

13. Become a Storyteller

"Let me tell the story of yesterday, and the night before," I wrote at the beginning of a journal entry one January day, when I was temporarily immobilized by a knee injury. "One January morning a little girl begged her mother to walk with her to the school bus stop. This was an unusual request coming from a daughter who had been proud to walk by herself for weeks. So the mother agreed both to please her daughter and out of curiosity…" The words I wrote led to an important discovery: writing in third person is an effective way to see events from another angle, another point of view. Writing as a story-teller requires a conscious step back from what is going on in your life, and puts yourself as the central character where you can observe the "action" more objectively. If there was a conflict between you and someone else, you may find yourself understanding and empathizing with the other after you have described the conflict from a neutral point of view.

Keep a journal. Write in it every day…. The great regret of my life is I didn't start keeping a journal from the age of sixteen on, even if only to read to one's children and grandchildren.
George Plimpton, Country and Abroad

14. Write your Memoirs

Journals are a gateway to writing memoir. As I became accustomed to daily writing, I found myself often associating events of the day with memories of my childhood, or refer-encing family stories I'd heard—often time and time again—growing up. Some of the stories were about me before I was old enough to remember them; others were "the time when" my brother, Mom, Dad, or others had a memorable, perhaps instructive, experiences. How surprising and enriching it is to discover new associations and meanings in old stories.

I developed a passion for writing short pieces of memoir with the notion of passing family stories onto my children, believing, as I do, that they would understand nothing of my background, so very different from their childhoods, unless I told them. In today's world, where the traditional family Sunday dinners and annual reunions among far-flung family members are not as feasible as in the past, writing down our stories is the only path open to those of us who wish to honor our ancestors and introduce them to our children.

Friday, October 18th

I was remembering as I worked raking leaves the time I spent as a kid playing in the apple orchard at the farm, and how I would dam up the brook and alter its course temporarily. These were happy times, being alone and sometimes with Mike [my brother], playing in the mud and gravel and water, surrounded by apple trees and the sounds and smells of the grass and fruit, the brook and the chickens in the poultry house. Are these memories responsible for my happiness moving rocks about today to make a garden path? Lifting up the slate in the north side to lay down on the east and south sides? What is it about a winding path that is so lovely and appealing?

15. Problem-solving

We cannot solve our problems with the same thinking we used when we created them.
Albert Einstein

One of the many rewards of journal writing is to realize that spooling out your thoughts and feelings on the page might expose and untangle knotty problems in your life. How this works I cannot say, but I can testify based on personal experience that it does so. I believe that problem-solving skills are not dependent upon minds that work mechanically or like a filing system. Answers to our questions are not always a matter of linear, logical thinking but rather of meandering, associative thoughts that lead to new ways of looking at a situation. The time you spend releasing thoughts and feelings onto the page and exploring your "stream of consciousness" will likely reveal insights you could never achieve by returning to your "old files," or staring into space cerebrating.

The strategy for problem solving assumes a clear understanding of the problem. You will need to flesh-out the scope and dimensions of your challenge before you can focus on how to solve it. As with whining, complaining, venting, when you edge toward a clearer comprehension of the problem you are facing, you are already approaching success in solving it.

One useful strategy for problem-solving is to begin with a stem sentence, such as "The problem is ..." and go on to describe the nature of your issues as simply as you can. Complex problems may have to be divided into several parts and include multiple responses to "The problem is" stem sentence. After setting your timer, scrawl quickly to override your conscious mind and break through your ordinary way of seeing things. Go on a rant. Say everything you have to say.

Your conclusion may be, "There's nothing whatsoever I can do about this," or you may begin thinking about half a dozen possible solutions. The important thing is that you recognize a problem and are able to devise ways to accept things as they are, minimize the effects upon you, take steps to eliminate it altogether, or seek advice from trusted loved ones or professionals.

You may be afraid you will get in over your head and into deep, murky water. That won't happen because you are not compelled to write about anything you do not want to. Stop if you are uncomfortable. Stop where you feel safe. You can tease out a solution at your own pace and in your own time, melding memories, thoughts, feelings, associations, and life experiences that will relieve your negativity and afford a resolution. At any point in the process, you may seek validation and guidance from trusted friends and care-givers.

Changing your way of looking at a troubling situation is a difficult and slow process. I have found that I need to exercise myself with new thoughts before I can begin to understand the trouble. I must describe the situation at length and at leisure, and at times, with humor, while my mind expands to incorporate larger possibilities than what I had earlier considered.

Sunday, June 13 10:36 am Deck

> *It takes discipline today for me to write here. I'm content to sit and stare into space, or to watch and listen to the birds. I don't know what to write that I haven't said a thousand times, or even once. I'm happy as I sit here, sweating in work clothes, the sun shining warm, the air now humid, and me on my second pot of coffee.*
>
> *... So, today I got up and planted portulaca by the low wall in front. I tried to intervene on behalf of a robin protecting its nest, which was under attack by a crow. This fight has continued on and off all morning. I saw the crow fly into the robin and hit it, like a body shot! I've thrown pinecones at the noisy, aggressive, evil crow, but basically feel foolish because I cannot change the nature of this conflict or its participants. I recall years ago going to the defense of a chickadee whose nest in the birdhouse hanging from the birch tree was being threatened by sparrows. I went out and stood underneath the birch tree with a broom to ward of the interlopers. How silly! When will I learn there are things I cannot control.*

16. Personal Crisis

Shocking news of any kind—a death, awful accident, frightening medical diagnosis, separation/divorce, a national or international crisis, such as, most recently, the Covid-19 pandemic—throws us off balance. We seek to find our center, comprehend what has happened, and find a way to cope.

Establishing the practice of journal keeping makes it easier to confide deeply upsetting experiences as they occur. Like meditation or prayer, the habit of journal writing strengthens you. As you are finding your way through a crisis, you have a trusted tool to help you cope, survive, and prevail over the circumstances.

Strong emotions urge us to take a deep dive into churning waters and racing currents within. At such times, you grab hold of your journal as if it were a lifeline to save you from drowning. In fact, your journal may be your lifeline.

My mother suffered a massive heart attack about ten years after I had started journaling. My parents were staying in Florida at the time. Dad called to tell me what had happened, how he'd gone out to the hardware store and returned to find Mom unconscious on the living room couch, had performed CPR, and called 911. There was little or no hope of recovery, he said. He had been unable to detect a pulse, and when he'd asked the paramedic riding in the ambulance with her to the hospital how she was, the medic had shaken his head and thrown his hands into the air. While I was en route from New York to Florida, I could only wonder if, when I arrived, Mom would be dead or alive.

Instinctively, before I left for the airport, I reached for a new blank book to carry with me to record my feelings and thoughts about this crisis. I wrote on the plane all the way to Florida. When I arrived at the hospital, I was told by nurses that Mom was regarded as a "miracle patient." The ambulance crew pronounced her dead, and the emergency room staff had pronounced her dead a second time. Then one of the doctors suggested they try to resuscitate her "one more time" using a drug in a dose that "might have killed someone half her age," according to her cardiologist, whom I spoke with the following morning. "It is a wonder she survived," he said. Her vital signs were restored, but there was no predicting at that moment if she would suffer permanent mental or physical impairments.

A nurse escorted me to Mom's room, where I expected to find her resting. Instead, she was sitting up as if waiting for a visitor, surrounded by consoles of blinking lights. She recognized me. "Mitzi! What are you doing here? It's so good to see you!"

We spoke briefly. The nurse reminded me I shouldn't tire her and that I could return the next morning at any time. I went back to Mom and Dad's house and wrote for as long as I needed to—pages and pages—about the emotional roller coaster I'd been on all day.

I stayed in Florida for three weeks to help out Dad, to take care of Mom, and to assist with her move from ICC to ICU, and then to a rehabilitation facility. Mom not only survived, she thrived. Her case was the talk of the hospital. Nurses, doctors and technicians came to visit her to see for themselves that she was alive. Her doctor proclaimed even her recovery a miracle. Although she had no memory of the day of the heart attack or her week in the hospital, and her right leg remained "wobbly" as a result of the heart damage, she was otherwise strong, sound, and as lively as ever in mind and spirit. We treasured her presence among us for another twelve years.

My journal helped me understand the cascade of emotions and thoughts that nearly overpowered me during those weeks in Florida, and it served another new and useful purpose. I took my journal to meetings with doctors and nurses, to consultations with social services and therapists, in order to keep the facts straight, to help me hear what was being said in a language I often did not fully understand unless I asked questions and wrote down the answers. With these notes, I was able to inform friends and relatives who were eager to hear news of Mom's condition. I believe my journal helped me keep myself together and made me a reliable correspondent as I connected with family members. I don't know how I could have survived that crisis without my journal.

To me, every hour of the day and night is an unspeakably perfect miracle.
Walt Whitman

17. Miracles and Coincidences

Coincidence is God's way of remaining
anonymous.
French proverb

Most of us could tell a story or two of a situation that seems to have had a miraculous, happy ending, and most of us have experienced startling coincidences. Use your journal to track and recall everyday coincidences and miracles you observe. It's likely that, if you reread your journal in the future, you will be surprised at how often you experience good fortune in the guise of a coincidence.

18. Prayers

Write down your prayers, perhaps in conjunction with a favorite poem, devotional meditations, scriptural readings, or newspaper headlines.

When I was on that plane to Florida, I did not set out to pray, but when I re-read those pages, I realized that much of what I wrote, though not in the form of a formal prayer, was nevertheless a plea for guidance, for strength, for comfort. I received all of that—and more. I received a miracle.

What sort of diary should I like mine to be?
Something loose knit and yet not slovenly, so
elastic that it will embrace anything, solemn, slight
or beautiful that comes into my mind. I should like
it to resemble some deep old desk, or capacious
hold-all, in which one flings a mass of odds and
ends without looking. I should like to come back,
after a year or two, and find that the collection
had sorted itself . . . into a mould, transparent
enough to reflect the light of our life.
Virginia Woolf

3.

How to Protect Your Privacy

*The births of all things are weak and tender;
and, therefore, we should have our eyes
intent on beginnings.*
Michel de Montaigne

◇◇◇◇◇◇◇

*K*eep your journal entirely to yourself until you choose to share it.

When you free yourself to write sincerely about anything at all, you must be free of the concern that someone might read what you have confided on your pages and misunderstand your intentions. If you are anxious about the possibility of someone reading your book without consent, you are imprisoning yourself, barring yourself from honest, forthright thought. Remember: You have the freedom to destroy what you have written whenever you choose.

With your newfound freedom of self-expression, you will find the pages of your journal a rich field in which you sow the seeds of fresh impressions and ideas. As in nature, the majority of your thought-seeds are likely to perish, but others will sprout and blossom into self-knowledge, new ways of thinking, an enlarged perspective on people and events and creative inspiration that will surprise you. You mustn't put all of this enriching potential in jeopardy! Protect your journal as you would valuable, vulnerable, fragile spring seedlings.

First, and most obviously, keep your journal in a safe place. Do not leave it openly displayed on tables or desktops to tempt a passerby to peek into your book. A safe place might simply be a drawer, or a safe-box. If you live in a busy household, you may need to be inventive. For example, store your journal inside a freezer bag tucked within a bag of vegetables inside a deep freeze, or bury it in a box of powdered laundry detergent. I know people who have hidden journals under loose floorboards in the garage attic, above a false-ceiling tile in the basement, and behind canned goods in the pantry. I know people who have written in code, and others who have written in another language to discourage snoops. A friend told me someone she knew who had taught himself to write backward to protect his journal from prying eyes. I know someone who stored a journal in a bank safety deposit box while going through a divorce.

I own 120-plus journals that have been protected in part by my atrocious handwriting. Often I struggle to decipher my own handwriting, so a curious reader of my journals is likely going to give up trying to decode my scribbles. This failure in penmanship was humiliating in third grade when my teacher gave me a *U*, meaning *unsatisfactory*, in penmanship on my report card. How ashamed I was! I could never have imagined back then that there is an upside to bad form.

I feel a need to protect innocent first-thoughts until they are mature enough to stand on their own. Here is a rather extreme example:

There was the time I took my kids and some of their friends to a movie and, once we were settled inside the theater, I started to worry that my car would be stolen. The car itself was a "station" car, a junker, but my journal was stashed under the front seat. *What would people think?* I wondered, *if they were to read my journal*? I imagined cruel, knee-smacking laughter and snide asides. As if! A car thief reading a journal? A car thief deciphering my handwriting? But I was not thinking. I was in a heart-thumping panic as I sat there with half a dozen youngsters in the front row of a dark movie theater. It was all I could do to sit still and not cause a disturbance by climbing over a row of moviegoers and racing to retrieve the journal from the car.

I stayed in my seat, but I could not concentrate on the movie. I was too frightened by the possibility of my rusted old car being stolen and my journal lost. When the house lights went up, I herded my charges up the aisle and out of the theater as fast as possible into the bright sunlight. The car was there. The journal was there. I exhaled in relief, and then was able to fully appreciate the company of excited children recounting the movie I had not really seen.

Twelve years later, I pulled that journal from a bookshelf and held it in my hands, remembering that movie theater incident. I was trying to decide whether to keep my old journals. How could I decide without reading them? To my surprise, that journal was fun to read. I was astonished and relieved that I wrote nothing to regret, and the writing wasn't *that* bad.

Over the years, I became less self-conscious. Releasing those inhibitions was frightening but also, of course, liberating. Over time I had grown more self-confident as a chronicler and witness to family activities, as well as to my own life. The routine recording of my thoughts in my journal improved my writing skills, too.

Later that same year I typed up that journal word for word, unedited, unexpurgated and unabridged—exactly as I had written it. My intention was to share honest observations, thoughts, feelings, and stories with my family. I had to type it to make it possible to read, but it is certainly not a formal piece of writing. I wanted to offer it as a model for my children, to show them it's all right to keep a crazy, sloppy, slipshod personal journal.

A Mother's Journal was at one time a tender and fragile thing. Over time, that journal and I became strong enough to stand alone and bear fruit. I gave copies of it, accompanied with pages of family photographs, to my kids at Christmas.

A second way to protect your privacy and enjoy peace of mind is to make a special bookmark for your journal. Copy the quote on the next page onto an index card or notepaper and keep it in your journal.

*We do not write in order to be understood; we
write in order to understand.*
Cecil Day-Lewis

◇◇◇◇◇◇

"I am trying to figure this situation out." I wrote these words on notepaper and stuck it in my book when I explored a thorny topic. "Forgive me if you read this and believe I'm wrong." Only then could I write with candid exuberance because, in the event I was hit by a bus or something, I had faith that anyone who found my journal loved me and knew that I loved him or her.

While we might feel at times that we are an emotional and psychological mess as we write, what we are doing is working out our issues word-by-word, phrase-by-phrase, and sentence-by-sentence, putting things in order as we put our words in order to complete our thoughts.

Our lives and our journals are ever-changing works-in-progress. As we write, we cannot know how our lives might change as a result of new insights, but we do know we are free to choose. Obviously, we cannot make a choice to claim or to discard a certain point of view or regard a new direction in our lives until we become conscious of our choices. To paraphrase Socrates, Life has greater worth if we take time to examine it.

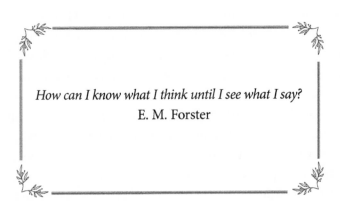

How can I know what I think until I see what I say?
E. M. Forster

4

Finding Times & Places to Write

It is not easy to find time to write. By far the most prominent theme of my early journals was to record again and again and *again* how I struggled to take the time to write. I persisted. A rhythm and routine for writing came—in time. Daily writing was a goal, not a reality, for several years—until my children were all in school. Often, even then, life got in the way.

Prepare to grapple. Patience and fortitude are essential for the practice of any discipline.

You will need to experiment with the time of day that suits you best. If you live in an active household, be on the alert and prepared to write when the moment presents itself. Imagine you're an athlete looking for a hole in the opposing defense, a space for you to run through, take a shot, and score.

The summer our family moved from New York City to Long Island, late in the evening when the children were in bed, I tried to recall just what I had done that day. Sometimes I could not remember! The days blurred together and I began to question myself: *Exactly what had I accomplished*? Was it enough just to have survived the day, kept the kids safe, and, I hoped, provided them with some good memories? What did I have to show for my efforts? Days later, I jolted awake, terrified by this thought: *What if I were to wake up in twenty years and, like Rip Van Winkle, look around and wonder what had happened while I was napping*? My children would be grown and I would have slept through their upbringing—and my life.

As any parent knows, it takes a lot of time and energy to keep an orderly home, to organize schedules, plan menus, shop for and prepare meals, watch over the kids, take an active role in the community, and so on. I'd become a stay-at-home mom and housewife, I was, for the first time since aged fourteen, officially unemployed! There was no indicator such as a personnel review, a raise, a promotion, to tell me how I was doing, and I could not define my goals or measure performance or progress.

I wanted to remember how I spent my days and my life. It was time to start keeping a journal! Though I earnestly tried to write each day, there were gaps as long as three months between entries during the first two years of journal keeping. Perhaps it is strange, but I never thought of giving up on the project, probably because I was getting more out of journal writing than I even knew. Still, I felt like a failure at the time for not managing things well enough to find five minutes to write.

After months of good intentions and stubborn determination to keep a record of family life, I learned to prepare for the odd moment that might turn up during the day, and I carried my journal with me. I learned to be prepared to log a few lines at any time, in any place—while standing in the basement waiting for the clothes dryer to stop, for example, or waiting for the kettle to come to a boil. I took my journal along in the car.

Early on, when I sat down to write, I seemed compelled to list all of the things I should be doing rather than writing. I felt guilty taking time away from chores even for a few minutes:

> January 22 10° F., 9:30 am
>
> I am torn in many directions as I sit here with valuable time. Should I put away the clean, folded laundry? Put the cans and bottles out in the garage? Finish cleaning up the kitchen? Do one more load of laundry to be completely caught up? Start dinner now, so we aren't tempted to spend extra money on a meal after skating? Write a half dozen Christmas cards and letters not yet completed, though the addressed envelopes are just inches away? Pay bills? Balance the checkbook? I've already sneaked in five minutes of stretching exercises, which I think are so important. My journal writing is maybe a similar stretching exercise, but for my brain.

I laugh, today, rereading this entry, realizing this list of chores is quite dated in 2021, and knowing that after listing to-dos, I let go of guilt and wrote for at least a few minutes. Maybe I was beginning to understand on some level that I *needed* to write. Journaling was not a luxury or self-indulgence; it was a necessity for me to have a time-out, to take "a breather" from my role as a wife and mother and to put things in perspective instead of getting carried away in a frenzy of never-ending activity.

To ease my guilty conscience, I efficiently set household products to work and let wet floors dry while I took a coffee break and wrote.

Thursday, September 21 10:05

As I write, the washer is chugging, the dryer is humming, and chemicals are attacking 'germs and stains' in the bathroom. From Katharine's room there are the sounds of busy gerbils shredding newspapers, and an occasional odd noise from the albino African frog, which is three times its original size and looks ready to burst through its skin.

When I started my writing practice and for the next six years or so, I awoke early in the morning (sometimes 4:30 am) and tip-toed to a bench near our front door where I could watch the sun rise and write the first thing that came into my sleepy head. More often than not, my reverie stopped as suddenly as it had begun with the sounds of a waking household.

Over the years of trying to fit writing into my daily schedule, there were plenty of days that I overslept, that I was up during the night for one or many reasons and could not rouse myself before the alarm trumpeted the start of the school and work day.

Fast-forward to today. My children are grown and my lifestyle is, of course, very different. I have no need to cook to please a crowd, no homework to check, no sports practices to drive to, and so on. My preferred writing time is still early in the morning between 5 and 6:00, and if I'm not in my armchair, I'm sitting up in bed with a lap desk on my knees. Today I enjoy a view of the dawning sky, treetops, and street traffic. Above a ceiling fan is whirring; my second cup of coffee is within easy reach. I'm writing with a teal blue pen, choosing it from among my collection of two dozen felt tipped pens displayed like a small bouquet in a favorite old coffee mug, and I'm in no particular rush. The one constant in all my journaling years is this: I avoid listening to the news or reading e-mail before I write. I cherish this time of day as I gently wake up to the world with my journal and my coffee.

Journal writing has sustained me from the early days of motherhood to present-day grandmotherhood, and I have prized every moment, difficulties and all. I've come to realize that striving to live consciously and noting each day is an expression of gratitude. When you review your journals, you will find that rereading, remembering, and reflecting upon memories is still more enriching.

Keeping a journal does not mean simply recording
the external facts of your life from one day to
the next. I'm talking about something that goes
much deeper. Journal writing is a process of vital
reflection that plunges you below the surface of
your life to its psychic roots. When you are writing
at that deeper level, your life itself changes.
Marlene Schiwy

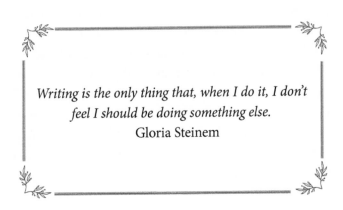

Writing is the only thing that, when I do it, I don't feel I should be doing something else.
Gloria Steinem

5

Writing for Healing, Health, & Wholeness

*O*nly after I'd been keeping a journal for many years did I learn that social scientists, medical clinicians, and educators have for decades been studying how writing helps us cope with diseases and difficult, even traumatic, situations to improve our overall health and wellbeing. I'd experienced first-hand that journaling is a safe place to organize my thoughts, vent emotions, and process information more thoroughly than I would otherwise have been able to, but it came as a surprise to learn of the growing range of benefits of writing about one's thoughts and feelings.

The first studies I read were those of social psychologist James W. Pennebaker, Ph.D., who is recognized as a pioneer in the study of the physical and psychological benefits of expressive/reflective writing. A professor at the University of Texas in Austin, Pennebaker's research finds that after subjects in a controlled experiment write about a troubling memory, measures of their vital signs improve: blood pressure drops, heart rate variability declines, breathing slows, and blood tests show an increased number of T-cells, which ward off disease by increasing the body's immunity. As recently as the summer of 2020, as I write, there is new reporting in the New York Times that people with higher numbers of T-cells are less susceptible to Covid-19.

Among Pennebaker's first experiments was an investigation of how writing about one's feelings and thoughts improves the health of people suffering from Post-Traumatic Stress Disorder (PTSD). He and dozens of other social scientists and medical clinicians around the world have, over many years, used a modified version of this experiment to study a wide range of illnesses, several of which I mention in this chapter.

In all of the studies I have read, writing is shown to have from a statistically negligible to a significantly positive effect on participants. None have reported negative effects. Some studies show immediate positive results; others indicate that benefits develop and even increase over a period of several months.

The conclusions of social science research may seem, in some cases, intuitive. When we sit down comfortably in a safe environment and pick up a pen to write in a journal, we might reasonably assume that we are relaxing, taking a break, and that the slowing down of our heart rate, breathing, and lowering of blood pressure are natural responses to a resting posture. Journal writers know that writing in a journal is not so much "braking" as it is "changing gears." Putting our lives into perspective by taking a step back to write about what is going on and how we feel relieves stress. Overall, the science suggests that reduced stress makes us writers less susceptible to stress-related diseases.

In rereading my old journals, I have come across passages like the one below that surprise me. I have no memory of the feelings that nearly overwhelmed me in the moment described.

9:50 study

The girls got off with a good hot breakfast of eggs and sausage, and packed lunches. I drove Lindsey. We are all tired and embattled with viruses, but so far fighting successfully.

I took my walk and, at the beach, found myself again so sad, so full of disappointment and feelings of futility that tears came to my eyes. I was ready to say, if anyone should have been there to ask, it was the cold and that made my eyes tear, but I knew different.

I think of how useless this journal writing may be. Why bother? Yet it is medicine for me, a medicine that seems to heighten all the painful symptoms until each makes me scream in fear or pain, and insists on being noticed, named, and treated in some way. The medicine is brutal, but if not taken in regular doses and swallowed and ingested, disease of my heart and spirit will surely overtake me. I would be unhappy and not know it or know why. It is better to be a human being, to try to be fully human, and to be conscious, and to know why one aches, and where.

People often ask, "Why me?" when disaster or disease strikes. We are angry and we want answers. Perhaps we do not have anyone to talk to about what is happening to us. Or, maybe we believe that we must be stronger than anyone else to protect our loved ones from the truth. For example, I know a woman who was diagnosed with breast cancer and who kept her condition entirely to herself. She even checked herself into the hospital for surgery and then called her family to say "not to worry," she would be home in a day or two and that she had made arrangements for meals and childcare. She believed she was doing what was best for her family. I know men who do not divulge their fears because they are supposed to be strong and just "fix" the problem without causing a fuss. None of us want our friends or relatives to worry, so we hold in our fears, anger, and doubts, and, consequently, we put ourselves under more stress.

Stress will not *disappear* if we write about our "deepest thoughts and feelings," as some studies instruct subjects; however, writing can *reduce* our stress and help us think more clearly. For example, reflecting upon a diagnosis, recalling our initial reaction to a diagnosis, confiding our hopes and doubts for the future on the page, seems to make us stronger and better able to take care of ourselves and our loved ones.

Human beings are storytellers. Storytelling is a way of comprehending our world and is as old as human history, as old as ancient stories of creation passed on orally to explain how the world came into being. We tell ourselves stories many times every day even though we are seldom aware of it. A "story" might come to mind in an instant and may be as simple as pausing for a moment to wonder: "Why didn't Dad answer the phone? Maybe he's out on a walk or having coffee with a neighbor? Hope he didn't fall."

We feel a need to know or, at the very least, to have a plausible explanation, for questions that come to mind. We might be prompted to investigate further—to call back in an hour or to phone the neighbor to see if Dad is there.

Most often we speculate, predict, or invent a reason why something "is" based on past experiences. When something shocks us—an automobile accident, a heart attack, a medical diagnosis—scientific research suggests that writing the story of what happened helps us integrate the new information and experience. We say after an automobile accident, for example, "What happened?" and then go about piecing together our memories of what we saw and heard before, during, and after the collision. We try to recognize responsibility or blame. We need a coherent story to explain to ourselves what happened and possibly why.

In 2007, a study was conducted with sixty-eight New England residents who had been diagnosed with metastatic breast cancer. The subjects were asked to write on three topics: (1) their experiences with the cancer, (2) their thoughts and feelings about not making a full recovery and facing death, and (3) any other traumatic experiences in life that may or may not relate to breast cancer. Each wrote for 20-30 minutes on four consecutive days.

The researchers concluded that patients' overall quality of life was improved by writing about the experience and the meaning of living with the cancer. Writing gave the women an opportunity to communicate their distress in ways that are often not possible in conversations with doctors, nurses, or loved ones. Writing seemed to help the women move ahead emotionally and arrive at a more positive understanding of their circumstances. Below is a quote from one of the participants in the study directed to the researchers:

"I would never have done this if you hadn't asked me. Now that I'm done, I see how great an experience it was. I learned a lot, and hope what I'm sending you will help. But, especially, I've learned that writing helps, and I will do it more in the future. Thank you for letting me have this wonderful opportunity."

Another study, which was conducted in England and published in 2011 by Lynn Willmott, Peter Harris, and others, explores the effects of expressive writing on 156 patients (131 men and 25 women) who had suffered their first heart attacks, or myocardial infarctions. In this study, participants were asked to write for three consecutive days for ten to twenty minutes about their thoughts and feelings with regard to having suffered a heart attack. They were asked specifically to describe how they might cope with their condition. For the final session, participants were instructed to "wrap things up" and summarize how their condition might affect them in the future. The control group was told not to write about emotions. A cardiac rehabilitation nurse was on standby to intervene if writing distressed the participants.

The findings of this study showed many positive results. Those who expressed their thoughts and feelings, as compared to the control group, subsequently had fewer visits to their doctors and hospitals in the coming five months, had attended more rehabilitation sessions, and required fewer prescriptive medications. Participants also had lower diastolic blood pressure, fewer cardiac symptoms, and "improved subjective mental well-being" in follow-up reports. The researchers concluded that writing about what had happened to them, telling the story of their heart attack, and describing their thoughts and feelings, helped patients develop a cognitive awareness of their health incident and an acceptance of necessary changes in lifestyle. The authors concluded:

"...This work is justified because if the potential benefits observed in this study are confirmed in other studies, then expressive writing may represent a low cost intervention to complement existing care post-MI [myocardial infarction]."

It appears that when we write the story of our experiences, including life-threatening illness, we are coming to terms with a "new reality" and feel more in control of our decisions and behavior.

Dozens of studies suggest that writing can help people who suffer serious or chronic pain from diseases such as sickle cell, rheumatoid arthritis, and fibromyalgia in a variety of ways, including helping patients communicate with medical professionals, who intimidate most of us, and with loved ones.

In an article titled "The Therapist's Voice," Judith Ruskay Rabinor, Ph.D. recalls listening to her English teacher recite words that changed her life: "We read to know we are not alone, we write to find ourselves." After first becoming an English teacher herself, Dr. Rabinor later became a psychologist and adopted writing as a tool for her clinical work with patients. She writes in her article:

"There is something about writing things down that is different from talking them out. Writing builds trust in one's ideas and beliefs. Writing makes you dig deep inside yourself. Writing reveals the self. Writing connects one to one's insides."

Many psychologists and counselors in a variety of special disciplines employ writing to complement their therapeutic approaches. In addition to areas of study already mentioned, I have read research articles that investigate the uses of writing in the treatment of victims of abuse, in marriage and family counseling, in grief counseling, and for those suffering from eating disorders, depression, and drug addictions.

Professional counselors, including therapists, psychologists, and social workers, adapt writing strategies to suit each client's specific needs. For example, sometimes clients are asked to write journals to share with the therapist because talking is too stressful for the patient. In some cases, a client is asked to write and then rewrite a story that disturbs him or her—for example, a deep regret for having made a mistake—to discover alternate meanings or explanations. In the case of facing regrets, for example, a client may come to recognize that the "regret" really had positive outcomes in the long term.

There are research articles about the use of journals in family and marriage counseling to help members of the family communicate. Often these days it is not possible to have regular family mealtimes, so families are counseled to keep a "common" journal on the kitchen table and to log in with a sentence a day just to say hello to family members and communicate what is going on in one's life. Communicating through a family journal allows a child to say, "I got 100 on my spelling test!" or, "Got into a fight at school." A parent might want to respond, "Sorry I got home too late and sorry about the fight. We'll talk tomorrow. Love you."

Common journals shared by a couple or a family are, obviously, not the same as personal journals, but the keeping of a common book of regular exchanges can keep family members somewhat up-to-date on each other's lives and suggest topics for later conversations.

Sometimes talking through "bad times" with a spouse is too challenging to put into words. It is more difficult to write than to talk, but we can clarify our thoughts, make our points, and remain calm in a written note; writing can open the door to conversation.

Journal writing is shown to have significant healing effects, yet personal writing is a great deal more than a remedy. Journal writing is an enjoyable way to learn to see the world and to recognize life's beauty and wonders. "The greatest thing a human being ever does in this world is to *see* something," wrote John Ruskin, an art critic in Victorian England. "To see clearly is poetry, prophecy and religion, all in one." For me, in addition to personal writing's capacity to heal our bodies, minds, and spirits, keeping a journal opens us to a new way of seeing.

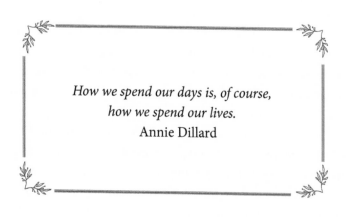

How we spend our days is, of course,
how we spend our lives.
Annie Dillard

6

Reading and Re-Viewing Old Journals

Weekly Review

A few years ago, I adopted a plan to review my journal entries every week, usually on a Sunday. I wish I had started this habit sooner.

Re-reading entries sharpens my memory of what happened the week before and gives me pause to savor and learn from experiences. Sometimes I use a marker to highlight the week's highs and lows, which inspires fresh ideas for planning the week to come. At other times, I use color-coded paper tabs to mark repeated intentions, observations, topics, then decide on a plan to do something or to let it go.

My journaling practices have changed, as will yours, over the years to adapt to life's circumstances. Nowadays I leave a blank page at the end of a week and a few blank pages at the end of a new journal for an index and year-end summary. To make it easier to find my weekly reviews as I flip through a journal, I write them in black ink and summarize the week in a numbered list on a single page. On the inside back cover I keep track of dates that are milestones.

I've been keeping journals for forty years, and there were things I discovered in my notebooks that I had forgotten about – like how my mother was attracted to my father and his hangdog look. Well, one of the reasons why he had a hangdog look then was because he had just been released from three months in prison for hijacking a truck. He thought it was full of cans of pork and beans, but it turned out to be buttons. I had forgotten that completely.

Frank McCourt

Annual Review

At about the same time I began weekly reviews, I began an end-of-the year tradition. In November, I begin skimming the year's journals by reading weekly reviews and searching out individual entries if I want more detail. By the holidays at the end of the year, I have a fresh appreciation for what the year has been like—major events, the peaks and valleys—for myself and my loved ones. I note major world and sporting events; favorite books and movies; new experiences; major purchases. I share reminiscences and important news of the year in holiday notes to people I am unlikely to write to at any other time. Often, I'm reminded of kindnesses I've received from friends, acquaintances, service providers, and sometimes strangers, and write a note of appreciation or give a small gift. Family conversations and time shared during Thanksgiving, Christmas, and New Year's celebrations are all the more poignant for having revived and shared a year of memories. Plus, I feel refreshed and ready to begin a New Year.

Reviewing your journals is satisfying for another all-important reason: nurturing the next generation. The times of your life take on new meaning and purpose when you read or tell your stories to the kids in your life, be they your children, grandchildren, nieces, nephews, or young friends. The real-life stories you pass on to children give them faith in themselves because they are equipped with special knowledge they will get nowhere else: survival stories of loved ones who have experienced the same challenges, joys, and hardships they are likely to face in their own lives. The children with whom you share your experiences will revere your tales and carry your stories and the lessons they teach with them into the future.

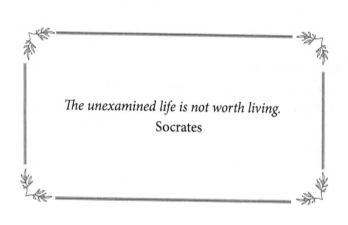

The unexamined life is not worth living.
Socrates

7

Journal Writing in the Classroom

Assigning journal writing to students helps them in at least two very important ways. First, regular writing improves reading and writing skills. Second, informal writing assignments develop essential critical thinking.

When I teach at the community college, I often assign a broad choice of topics for students to focus on in a personal journal. A student might decide, for example, to write an autobiography, a biography of a relative, a memoir, or a series of personal responses to works of literature and art. I urge students to experiment with various sentence structures, and to practice using the right synonym for a particular word. I ask ESL writers to describe their daily routines, the members of their family, their educational and career goals. Older college students are challenged to translate favorite poems or passages from their language into English. Students are given credit for maintaining a journal, but I do not grade them. I correct my students' work only if they wish me to. Though the bulk of their journal-keeping is done at home or in the library, we spend a few minutes in each class writing. After all, many of the students also have full time jobs and families to support. Ten minutes in class may be the only time all day students have to write.

Critical thinking skills are essential to one's success and happiness, but most students fall into one of two groups: Some are hesitant to speak up because they don't know what they think and fear criticism; others speak up too often before they have thought through their ideas. By writing a reaction to a work of literature, an introverted student can take his or her time quietly working out the development of his thoughts before laying claim to them formally in expressing an opinion or taking a stand in an essay. Similarly, an extroverted student who might seem to think more quickly and assuredly will discover weaknesses in his point of view if instructed to analyze his work and identify logical fallacies.

Critical thinking is essential not only to academic success but also to managing the day-to-day complexities of life. We must all learn to discern truth from falsehood, claims from evidence, and passionate beliefs from well-reasoned arguments. Reading posts on social media, listening to podcasts and broadcasts, analyzing speakers' rhetoric and "where they are coming from" is essential to making the right choices in our lives.

Journal writing helps all of us discover what we think and how we feel, which is how we prepare ourselves to act in the world. In other words, the better we understand ourselves, the better equipped we are to listen to others. This is the process by which we develop mutual understanding and empathy. Knowing ourselves, listening to others, synthesizing points of view based on logical thinking and precise language, and having the strength to maintain our own straight thinking is preparation for civil discourse and participation in the community. Journal writing can help prepare the leaders of tomorrow.

8

Where Do Your Journals Go When You Die?

An Argument for Giving Journals Away

My children are due to inherit all of my journals. I have talked to my kids and written a letter suggesting that the books be divided among the three of them, or just removed to the local incinerator. The letter is included in a folder with my will, power-of-attorney, and other documents pertaining to my death. I trust my children to do what is best from their point of view, and have absolved them of guilt. We are a practical family who live in small to average-sized spaces. We are also a far-flung family, and each of us moves rather frequently. Lugging around cartons of journals is impractical and expensive.

I also leave open the possibility that, not withstanding the illegible handwriting, I will donate the whole lot to a library or institution, several of which have cropped up recently for the purpose of preserving everyday-life memories. How astonishing this is to me, but of course this is not the first time that my journal writing habit has astonished me. My journals were initially entirely private property, yet now I am willing to consider sharing them with the world.

What accounts for my 180-degree change in perspective toward protecting the privacy of my journals? The answer is that I know, now, that nothing I have experienced or felt or thought about in my lifetime is different from any other human being. If my journals might be of interest, encouragement, or comfort to someone else, I would freely offer them.

An Argument for Destroying Journals

Perhaps in the future I will decide to destroy my journals. While I began writing with the intention of recording my children's lives from my point of view, my journal soon became a repository of *my* experiences, thoughts, and feelings. My books contain many prized stories about my daughters, yet my journals are essentially about my life, not theirs. My hope is to cull worthwhile stories about our lives together before I die, and then throw away my journals.

My maternal grandmother, born in 1894, destroyed her journals. She kept a neat row of journals on the narrow shelves of her oak secretary-desk in her farmhouse in northwestern Ohio. Most of these slender books had black covers with red or black spines stamped *Record* or *Journal* in gold letters. The books were accounts for the farm, including the chickens and milk cows that she tended. She wrote down the cost of chicks and feed, for example, and the income from eggs. Grandma noted diseases that spread through the flock, severe weather, and the cost of materials for repairs to buildings and fencing.

Hidden in plain sight among the rows of farm accounts and cookbooks were journals where Grandma wrote about her life and family. I did not know these journals existed until I found Grandma burning them in her backyard one autumn day in 1968. I was on a visit home from college, and made my customary stop to say hello. She was behind her house pitching journals, one-by-one, into a blazing burning-barrel, a common way to dispose of trash and yard debris back then. I asked her if I could look at one of the half dozen books she held stacked in her hands. The ruled pages were written from the top to bottom of the page in neat cursive handwriting.

"Why are you burning these up, Grandma?"

"There is no use keeping them," she said. "There are things in there that might hurt people's feelings. Things that might be embarrassing."

It never occurred to me to persuade my grandmother to change her mind because I had been taught not to question or argue with my elders. But how I wish, now, that I had tried to talk Grandma out of destroying those books. They would have been a priceless legacy. Grandma, who left school after completing eighth grade, as did most farmwomen of her generation, was the wisest person I know. Shy, humble, and sensitive about her lack of formal education, she once told me, "You know more already than I'll ever know."

Surely my grandmother's life was every bit as busy as my own. She not only raised three children, but she had cows to milk every morning and every evening, chickens to feed and tend to, a house and garden to keep up. She helped Grandpa manage their eighty-acre farm. I have photos of her driving a tractor. How did she do it all?

My grandparents were active members of Pleasant Hill

Methodist Church and the local grange. I don't remember seeing either of them idle. Even when she sat down, she was moving: rocking an oak rocking chair, crocheting, or peeling potatoes. Her only entertainment was music, and the farmhouse shook when she played hymns and popular tunes on the upright piano in the parlor.

My mother was born in 1918, and her family survived the Spanish Flu pandemic. What precautions did they take? How did it affect the extended family and neighbors in rural Allen County? How did Grandma find time to record in her journals? How I wish I knew.

I regret I don't have one of Grandma's journals, and for that reason, I'm persuaded—at this moment, at least— that I'll pass on my journals to my daughters. I am confident they will make the right decision.

~~

9

Epilogue

Write every day or as often as you possibly can . . .

You are invited to write the last chapter of this book. The space on the following pages is provided for you to practice writing *A Book of My Own*. On days you need encouragement or inspiration, read—silently or aloud— Brenda Ueland's advice to writers:

"Write every day or as often as you possibly can, as fast and carelessly as you possibly can, without reading it again, anything you happened to have thought, seen or felt the day before. In six months look at it . . . . You will see that what you have written with the most slovenly freedom — in those parts there will be vitality, brilliance, beauty."

10

A Book of My Own

by

_____

_____
_____
_____
_____
_____
_____
_____
_____
_____
_____
_____
_____
_____
_____

_____

_____

_____

_____

_____

_____

_____

_____

_____

_____

_____

_____

_____

_____

_____

_____

_____

_____

_____

_____

_____

_____

_____

_____

_____

_____
_____
_____
_____
_____
_____
_____
_____
_____
_____
_____
_____
_____
_____
_____
_____
_____
_____
_____
_____
_____
_____
_____
_____
_____

Acknowledgments

"I am part of all that I have met," wrote Alfred Lord Tennyson in his poem, "Ulysses". In that spirit I say "thank you" to family near and far, to friends past and present, to colleagues, students; to all those with whom I have spent time in a classroom or workshop. We share and enhance one another's lives—and work.

Specific individuals prompted me to write this book. At Stony Brook/Southampton, Robert Reeves encourages writers to take on challenges, to take risks; Lou Ann Walker, my thesis adviser, guides writers with creative ideas, insights, and good humor; Susan Worley Kaufman, head librarian at the Southampton campus, helped me assemble dozens of research articles.

Professors Elaine Preston, David Moriarty, Joseph Inners, and Michael Boecherer, my colleagues at Suffolk Community College in New York, are a lasting inspiration and examples of extraordinary, dedicated teachers and administrators working tirelessly on behalf of all students as well as the wider community.

To the memory of Madeleine L'Engle: Her journals first sparked my belief that I, too, could be a mother and a writer.

To Christina Baldwin: I happened upon her book, *One to One*, years after beginning journaling when my enthusiasm was flagging. Her book motivated me to persevere in the discipline, and I am forever grateful.

To Susan Tieberghien, whose lectures and books deepened my appreciation for the habit of journal writing and opened my eyes to the spiritual attributes of personal writing

To Sarah Ban Breathnach, whose books on creativity, writing, and home-making helped me hold it all together

To the memory of Tilly Olsen, whose classic book, *Silences*, describes the struggle everyone must fight if we are to release and develop our unique creative spirits.

To my steadfast friends and writing cheerleaders, Antoinette Truglio Martin and Jacqueline Goodwin.

To Kathie Collins and Paul Reali, co-founders of The Charlotte Center for Literary Arts (CharlotteLit), who welcomed me into the Charlotte writing community.

To top-notch editor, Betsy Thorpe, whom I met at one of the many excellent workshops at CharlotteLit.

To Diana Wade, a talented and patient book designer.

Dear Readers and Writers,

I would like to hear from you and welcome your feedback. I'm available to facilitate writing workshops based on this book. Write to me at WirtPublishing@gmail.com.

May your writing continue always to nourish you with joy, peace of mind, and personal growth.

Melinda L. Ferguson

About The Author

Melinda L. Ferguson was born and raised in Lima, Ohio. After graduating from Miami University of Ohio with a BA in English, she moved to New York City where she earned a Masters' Degree from Columbia University, and worked as an editor at several publishing companies including Warner Books, Walker & Co., and Macmillan. In the 1990s, her family moved to Northport, NY on Long Island, where she facilitated workshops in memoir and journal writing at libraries and adult education centers. For many years she served as an Adjunct Professor of English at Suffolk County Community College. In 2016, she was awarded an MFA degree in Creative Writing & Literature from Stony Brook/Southampton University. In 2019, Melinda moved to Charlotte, NC, to teach at Central Piedmont Community College and at Charlotte Center for The Literary Arts (CharlotteLit), a non-profit organization supporting literary arts and culture.

Lightning Source UK Ltd.
Milton Keynes UK
UKHW012016020921
389944UK00001B/137